LEVEL 4

Re-told by: Paul Shipton
Series Editor: Melanie Williams

Pearson Education Limited
Edinburgh Gate, Harlow,
Essex CM20 2JE, England
and Associated Companies throughout the world.

ISBN: 978-1-4082-8867-2

This edition first published by Pearson Education Ltd 2012

1 3 5 7 9 10 8 6 4 2

Text copyright © Pearson Education Ltd 2012
Copyright © 2012 Disney Enterprises, Inc. and Pixar.
Slinky® Dog is a registered trademark of Poof-Slinky, Inc. © Poof-Slinky, Inc.;
Mr. and Mrs. Potato Head® are registered trademarks of Hasbro, Inc. Used with permission. © Hasbro, Inc.;
Mattel and Fisher-Price toys used with permission. © Mattel, Inc. All rights reserved.

The moral rights of the author have been asserted
in accordance with the Copyright Designs and Patents Act 1988

Set in 17/21pt OT Fiendstar
Printed in China
SWTC/01

All rights reserved; no part of this publication may be reproduced, stored in a retrieval system,
or transmitted in any form or by any means, electronic, mechanical, photocopying,
recording or otherwise, without the prior written permission of the Publishers.

Published by Pearson Education Ltd in association with
Penguin Books Ltd, both companies being subsidiaries of Pearson Plc

For a complete list of the titles available in the Penguin Kids series please go to www.penguinreaders.com.
Alternatively, write to your local Pearson Longman office or to: Penguin Readers Marketing Department,
Pearson Education, Edinburgh Gate, Harlow, Essex CM20 2JE, England.

Years ago, Andy played with his toys every day. His favorite toys were Woody the cowboy and Buzz the space ranger.

But now Andy was older. It was time for college.

Andy put all his toys in a big, black bag. After he left, they could go in the attic. Andy only wanted to bring Woody with him to college.

Later, Andy's mom saw the bag outside Andy's room.

She thought it was trash, but really it was Andy's toys. She took the bag outside.

Woody watched her from the door of Andy's room.

"Oh, no!" he said. "Andy's mom is making a mistake. That bag is for the attic. It isn't trash! I must save my friends!"

The toys got out of the trash bag and into a box with SUNNYSIDE on it.

"Jump out!" Woody cried.

"Perhaps the Sunnyside Daycare Center is better for us," said Buzz.

"No! Andy's mom made a mistake!" cried Woody.

Suddenly, Mom shut the car door. But Woody was in the car, too!

Mom drove to Sunnyside Daycare Center.

At the daycare center, a teacher took the box of toys to one of the classrooms. There were a lot of toys there.

"Welcome to Sunnyside!" said a pink bear. His name was Lotso.

Andy's toys liked this place.

"We can have a new life here," Jessie said.

"Let's stay!" cried Slinky Dog.

But Woody was not happy.

"We're Andy's toys," Woody said. "We *must* go home!"

He was angry because his friends did not follow him to the door.

Woody ran out of the classroom. What was the best way for him to leave?

He climbed through a window and up to the roof. He could not jump from here, but then he saw a kite.

"I can fly!" said Woody.

He held the kite and *jumped*. The kite flew up over Sunnyside's walls.

But suddenly the kite fell down into a tree. Now Woody could not move.

A little girl from the daycare center saw him in the tree. Her name was Bonnie. Bonnie took Woody and put him in her bag.

At Sunnyside, Andy's toys were excited about their new life.

But then the children ran into the classroom. These children were very young. They did not know how to play with the toys. They dropped them and threw them. They hit them and hurt them. They painted with them. They tried to *eat* them!

"This is terrible!" said Buzz.

That night Buzz climbed out of the classroom.

"Lotso's nice. He can move us," Buzz told the other toys.

But Lotso was not nice now. "*You* can stay with us in our nice classroom," he told Buzz. "But your friends must stay with the little children!"

"No!" cried Buzz.

Lotso told the Sunnyside toys to push Buzz to the floor.

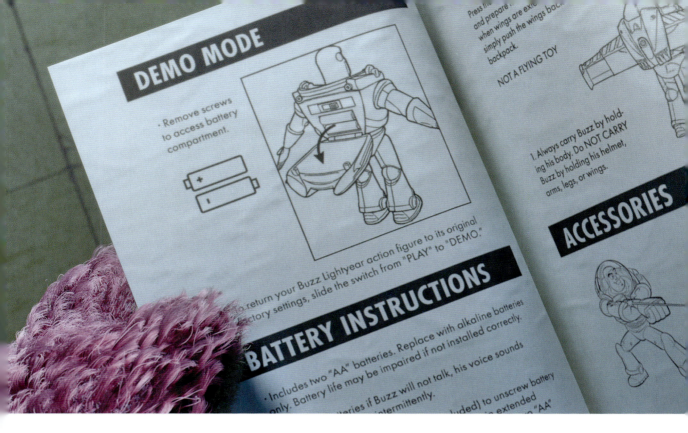

"Move the switch on his back," Lotso said.

After the toys moved the switch, Buzz could not remember his name or friends.

Lotso took Buzz back to his old classroom.

"We're leaving," said Jessie.

"No!" Lotso said.

"Who's going to stop us?" asked Jessie.

Suddenly, Buzz jumped out! He listened only to Lotso now. He stopped his old friends easily.

"Now put them all in prison!" Lotso said.

Buzz and the Sunnyside toys put Andy's toys in toy baskets.

"Buzz!" cried Jessie. "We're your friends!"

But Buzz did not remember her now.

"You new toys must learn about life at Sunnyside," Lotso said. "Now sleep well, because tomorrow the little children are going to play with you again!"

Woody was at Bonnie's house. Her toys were nice, but Woody wanted to go home.

"Are your friends there?" asked one of Bonnie's toys.

"My friends are at Sunnyside," answered Woody sadly.

"Sunnyside? That's the *worst* place!" cried Bonnie's toys in surprise.

Woody listened to all their terrible stories about Sunnyside.

He *had* to go back and help his friends.

The next morning Woody hid inside Bonnie's bag. At Sunnyside he climbed out and ran back to the old classroom.

He watched the little children playing. Bonnie's toys were right — this *was* a terrible place. After the children left, Woody ran to his friends.

"Woody!" they cried happily.

Woody smiled. "We're going to leave *tonight*," he said.

Before the toys could leave, there was a problem – Buzz.

"What's he saying?" Jessie said. "I don't understand him."

But Woody had a plan.

"Now!" he shouted.

The toys jumped on Buzz. Woody moved the switch on the space ranger's back.

Buzz looked up. "What's happening?" he asked.

"You came back!" cried Jessie.

"Yes," said Buzz. "Where was I?"

The toys ran outside into the garden of the daycare center. It was very dark.

Woody pointed to a garbage chute in one of the walls.

"That's the only way out," he said.

The toys started to move carefully across the garden. They did not want any of Lotso's toys to hear them.

Soon they were at the chute.

The toys were afraid because the chute was dark. What was at the bottom?

"Come on!" said Woody, and he jumped.
The toys followed him.

There was a dumpster at the bottom.

"We have to jump across it," cried Woody.

But suddenly, Lotso was there. The Sunnyside toys were with him. "Where are you all going?" the bear asked angrily.

"We're going home to Andy," said Woody.

"Andy doesn't love you!" shouted Lotso. "Children don't *really* love their toys!"

Big Baby started to cry. He was one of the Sunnyside toys.

"It's true!" shouted Lotso at him. "Your child didn't love *you*!"

Big Baby was angry now. He took Lotso in his arms and threw him into the dumpster!

Woody, Buzz, and their friends ran for hours and hours. They arrived at Andy's house early in the morning.

The toys jumped into a box with the word ATTIC on it. Only Woody stayed on the floor.

"Goodbye, Woody!" said all the toys.
"Have a good time at college with Andy!"

Woody climbed into a box with COLLEGE on it.

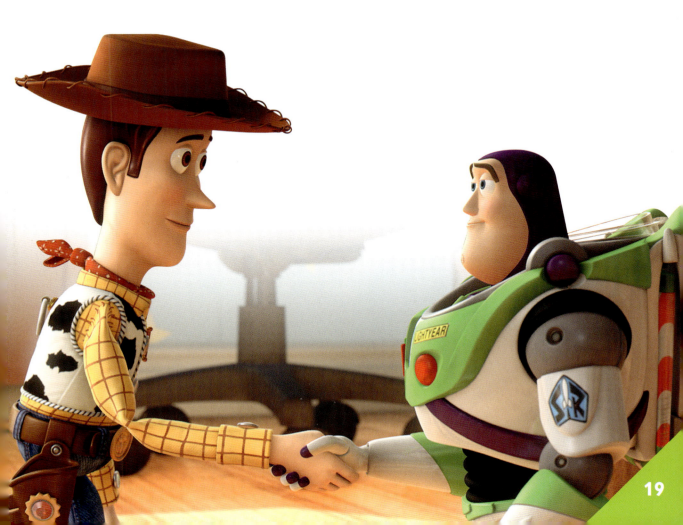

Andy and his mom came into the room. Mom started to cry.

"It's okay," Andy said. "I'm going to love college!"

Inside the box, Woody understood.

After Andy and Mom left, Woody jumped out. He wrote a new name and address on the box with ATTIC on it.

Andy came back and read the address on the box.

Andy thought his Mom wanted him to give the old toys to her friend's daughter.

Andy drove to the address on the box. It was Bonnie's house.

Andy showed the toys to Bonnie. "These were my toys," he told her. "I want you to have them now."

Andy and Bonnie played with the toys.

Then Andy stood up. He had to drive to college.

Woody looked at Andy and remembered all the good times.

"Now we're going to have good times with Bonnie," said Buzz to his old friend.

It was true. This was the start of a happy new life for the toys.

Activity page 1

Before You Read

1 Match the words and pictures.

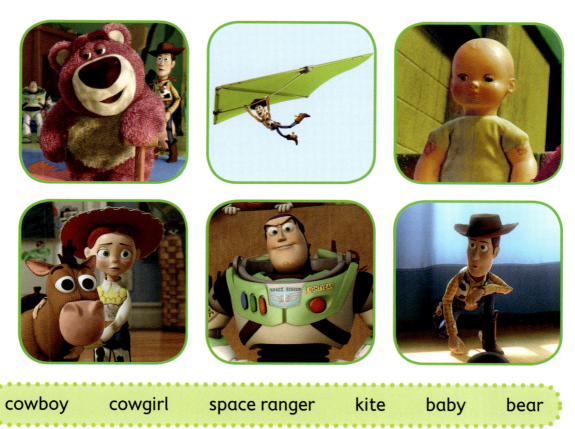

cowboy   cowgirl   space ranger   kite   baby   bear

2 Where are the toys in the first picture on page 7?
Choose the right answer.
   a   in a toy store
   b   in a classroom
   c   in a house

Activity page ❷

After You Read

❶ Read and write True (T) or False (F).
1 Andy wanted to give his old toys to the daycare center. (page 3)
2 Mom made a mistake with the bag of toys. (page 4)
3 All Woody's friends wanted to stay at the Sunnyside Daycare Center. (pages 6 and 7)
4 Woody left the daycare center by kite. (page 8)
5 Woody went from the daycare center to Andy's house. (page 13)

❷ Put these sentences in the right order.
a Buzz could not remember his friends.
b Woody climbed up to the roof of the daycare center.
c Andy gave his toys to Bonnie.　7
d Bonnie took Woody to her house.
e Mom took Andy's toys to the daycare center.　1
f Woody came back to the center for his friends.
g Big Baby threw Lotso in the dumpster.

❸ Draw a picture of the toys' new life at Bonnie's house.
Write one or two sentences about it.